FOLENS

Citizenship and

PSHE

BOOK ONE

Eileen Osborne & Steph Yates

Contents

To the reader

What's this book about?
You might find that question hard to answer just by looking at the chapter headings. After all, what has Keeping Clean got to do with the Houses of Parliament? The answer is YOU. This book is about you. It's about you as an individual, you as part of a family, you as part of the communities to which you belong and you as an active citizen in the twenty-first century. It's also about the people around you and about the United Kingdom as a whole. That's quite a lot to fit into one book.

What can this book teach me?
There are probably plenty of facts and figures in this book that you don't yet know. For example, do you know how many MPs there are in the UK or how many cells make up a human being? But this book is not really about facts and figures – it's more about forming your own opinions and learning to understand people and how they work, play and live together. To get the most out of it, you need to think about the topics, listen to other people's views, and be prepared to discuss your own ideas. If you let it, this book can help you to get on with yourself and other people better – and that's quite a lot to achieve.

How will I use the book?
Your teacher will guide you through the lessons. Sometimes you will be writing and this could be notes, diagrams, stories, letters, plays or other types of writing. Sometimes you will be talking, either sharing your ideas, making plans or working in role as another character. You will also have chances to find out more by carrying out research and this may involve looking through books, newspapers or using the Internet. That's quite a lot of activities.

Why are these lessons important?
These lessons are important because **you** are important, and the people around you are important. Anything that helps us understand each other and live together peacefully is important. That's quite enough for now.

Eileen. Steph.

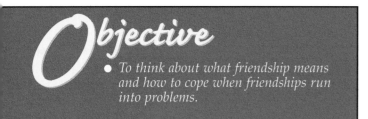

Objective
- To think about what friendship means and how to cope when friendships run into problems.

You and your friends

1. Write down eight statements about friends, beginning with the words 'A friend ...'. The two examples below may help you to start.

A friend cheers me up when I'm feeling down.

A friend always sticks up for me, no matter what.

2. Put your eight statements into order, beginning with the most important ones. Do other people agree with your order?

CONSIDER

3. Most friendships run into problems from time to time. Look at the cartoons below. What are the problems? Is anyone to blame? How could they be dealt with? Choose one of the cartoons, role-play the situation and continue it, showing how the problem could be dealt with.

I know we are friends but you can't keep copying my homework. You never used to.

If you don't let me, I'll tell everyone that secret you told me.

Is Saskia coming out to play?

I'm sorry, she's out with friends.

She never wants to play with me any more.

Why don't we invite Hannah and Jill? We could go in a group for once.

No, let's go on our own.

FACT TO THINK ABOUT ... FACT TO THINK ABOUT ... FACT TO THINK ABOUT ...

In a recent survey, 87% of 18–21-year-olds were still in touch with friends from when they were 11.

KEY WORDS   best friend   fair-weather friend   gang   peer group

DISCUSS

4. In pairs, write a few sentences describing a friendship problem one of you has had, or has heard about, but don't include anyone's name. Your teacher will read out each problem. As a class, group the problems under headings showing the sorts of things that can upset a friendship. The headings below may be useful as a starting point.

> New person arriving.   Having different interests.   Nasty rumours.

BRAINSTORM

5. Sometimes friends can sort out problems between themselves but, at other times, they may need outside help. Brainstorm a list of people or groups, such as an older sister or Childline, who could help sort out friendship problems.

6. Who might be able to help the people below?

My friend tells me things about her mum that worry me. I think her mum is drinking too much.

Alec says he's my friend but he keeps calling me names. It's really doing my head in.

I feel really lonely since I moved to this town. I have no real friends here.

7. Design a leaflet about the pleasures and problems of friendship, including advice on dealing with problems.

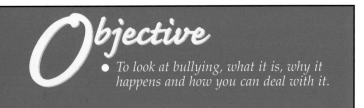

Dealing with bullying

CONSIDER

1. What is the difference between bullying and having a laugh? Sometimes bullying is difficult to spot. Look at the situations below. Could they be bullying? How could you tell?

Hey Dumbo! come and play football.

Kerry can work with us Miss.

I don't want to.

BRAINSTORM

2. Brainstorm examples of bullying. Then write a definition for the word 'bullying'.

3. Read the statements below and say whether you agree or disagree with each part. What makes someone bully others? What makes someone more likely to become a target?

Bullies are usually:	**Targets are usually:**
aggressive	weak
strong	clever
unhappy at home	easily forgiving
poor at school work	different from other people
people who enjoy hurting others.	caring.

DISCUSS

4. The boxes below show two ways of dealing with bullying. Discuss each method and say what the advantages and disadvantages might be.

Frogging
Every time you are insulted you say, "Yes, that's true" or "Yes, you might be right". By 'eating up the insults' like this, the bully cannot hurt you and has to give up.

No blame approach
The bully and the target sit down with a third person, who may be a counsellor, teacher or trained older student. They both say how they feel and consider how the situation could be improved. No one is blamed; the conversation focuses on their feelings and ways forward.

FACT TO THINK ABOUT ... FACT TO THINK ABOUT ... FACT TO THINK ABOUT ...

Each year, between 10 and 12 children in the UK kill themselves because of bullying.

KEY WORDS | bullying   target   assertiveness   conciliation

CONSIDER

5. Look back at your brainstorm on types of bullying. For each item, suggest ways of dealing with it at the time and afterwards.

6. Now read the news article below. List the people who could have done something to avoid the situation getting out of hand. What could each one have done?

THE DAILY NEWS

Fur Flies at Fuddlestone High

The Headteacher of Fuddlestone High School defended his decision to exclude Anita Mark earlier this week. Anita was excluded for hitting another 11-year-old girl who, we are told, is too frightened to return to school after the attack. Anita feels the exclusion is unfair. She told reporters, "That girl has bullied me all term. She calls me names, steals my things, tells lies about me and pushes and kicks me. I told my teacher and Head of Year and they spoke to her but it carried on. My mum even went up to the school but it made no difference. Dad said I should stand up for myself, so when she pushed me in the corridor I hit her twice." The headteacher says that he expects both girls to be back in school next week and added, "I hope things will be able to get back to normal."

ROLE–PLAY

7. In groups, role-play a 'no blame' session with a counsellor, the two girls from the article and their parents.

8. It isn't just children who bully. Adults can bully children or other adults. Anyone can find themselves a target of bullying. Write a set of guidelines to help someone who finds they are being bullied.

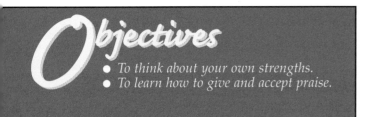

Objectives
- To think about your own strengths.
- To learn how to give and accept praise.

Praising you, praising me

CONSIDER

1. Think about a time when you did something well and were praised for it. How did you feel? What do you say when someone praises you?

2. Everyone needs praise and sometimes it's good to praise ourselves. Write down your six best qualities. The ideas below may help you. Show them to someone who knows you well and see if they agree or disagree with your opinion of yourself. When you have listened to them, make any changes to your list that you think are needed.

3. Swaylee is designing himself a Boaster Poster. He is writing and drawing about six things that he has done in the last year for which he is proud. Look at Swaylee's ideas, then design a Boaster Poster for yourself.

Research shows that people perform better if they are praised, particularly if they are told what they have done well, rather than just being told 'well done'. Constant and ill thought-out praise does not work.

KEY WORDS | praise   constructive criticism   self-esteem

When you praise yourself you have to be honest, and the same is true when you praise others. In most situations, there is something positive you can say. PET praise is best – praise that is Precise, Earned and True.

Precise – pinpointing the actual thing that is being praised. Not just 'well done'.

Earned – given because somebody has made an effort. 'You've got nice eyes' is a compliment, but it isn't really praise.

True – 'That was a delicious meal' might be polite but it's not real praise if you hated every mouthful.

I let in seventeen goals

Yes, but if you hadn't stopped that last one with your teeth, it would have been eighteen

4. Giving genuine praise can be as embarrassing as receiving it. Practise giving praise by writing two praise notes like the ones shown. One should be to someone who is in your class now and the other should be for an adult who you will see within the next week.

To: Emily
From: Tom
I really liked the way you helped Jack when he couldn't find the classroom last week.

To: Mrs Farmer
From: Sam
Thank you for giving me the chance to explain why I hadn't finished my homework. It was very kind and understanding of you.

5. Give your praise note to the person in your class and, before next week, give the other praise note out. How did people react to being praised? Is public praise better than private praise?

CONSIDER

6. Sometimes, being honest means looking at the bad points about yourself as well. Think of something you need to improve, then set yourself a target to aim for. Write yourself a praise note that you can give yourself when you achieve your target.

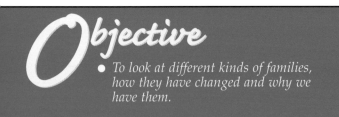
Families

BRAINSTORM

1. Brainstorm reasons for having families. Which of the reasons are emotional and which are practical?

DISCUSS

2. Families are often in the news. Discuss each of the headlines below. What do you think the stories are about? Do you think the headlines are fair?

Marriage is now out of date

Single mums responsible for falling moral standards

Children of violent parents become violent parents themselves

Teenage pregnancies due to parents not teaching their children about sex

No one loved me so I stole, claims 14-year-old burglar

Children of working mothers do badly at school

3. Families in Britain have changed over the years. Study the table on page 11, then describe two families, one from 1900 and one from 2000. Your descriptions should include who is in the family, their ages, what they do, how they get on with each other, and any other important information.

FACT TO THINK ABOUT … FACT TO THINK ABOUT … FACT TO THINK ABOUT …

Seven per cent of divorced or separated fathers have custody of their children.

KEY WORDS | lone-parent family   stepfamily   married   blended family   adopted   fostered

1900	2000
Contraception was unavailable so families often had as many as ten or twelve children. Poorer medical care meant that many children and babies died.	Most families have far fewer children, but those that are born are likely to be healthier and live longer.
Divorce was almost unheard of.	42% of marriages end in divorce.
Most people having children would have been married to each other, or would have married when the woman became pregnant.	Many couples live together without being married, or have children without living together.
Women tended to begin having children in their twenties or earlier.	Contraception means that people can choose to start their families much later, or choose not to have children at all.
Lone-parent families resulted from the death of one partner.	Far more lone-parent families occur due to divorce or having children without being in a long-term relationship.
Children were sometimes brought up by grandparents, aunts or other relatives, particularly if the mother had to work. Large orphanages or poor houses looked after others.	Children may still be brought up by other relatives. They may also be adopted or fostered by new families. A few children live in small homes where trained staff care for them.
People sometimes remarried if a partner died.	Many parents remarry or move in with new partners who may have children of their own. This creates stepfamilies or 'blended' families, where children from different relationships live together.

CONSIDER

4. Some people think that families are dangerous, because children can be badly treated without anyone knowing and also because children learn bad habits from their families, which they then pass on to their own children. They argue that children should be brought up in groups with specially trained adults who have learned about child development and child care. List the advantages and disadvantages of families. Do you think we should keep them?

5. Describe a typical family of the year 2100.

Family pressures

CONSIDER

1. Read the play below. Which characters do you have sympathy for? Why?

Thursday morning in the Armstrong household. Characters: Mr Armstrong, Mrs Armstrong, Amy aged 14, Daniel aged 12.

Mrs A: Hurry up Daniel! I want the bathroom.

Daniel: OK.

Mr A: Janet, is my white shirt clean? I've got a meeting.

Mrs A: Look in the washing basket. You'll have to iron it. Have you had breakfast Amy?

Amy: Mmm?

Mrs A: Have you had breakfast? And why are you wearing those earrings? You can't wear those to school. Honestly Amy, if it's not make-up it's jewellery. Take them out now!

Amy: Sarah wears them and Mrs Wood never says a word.

Mrs A: I don't care what Sarah does. They're not allowed and they're not safe. Take them out and put your studs in and have some breakfast.

Daniel: Can I have my pocket money today?

Mrs A: No. I get paid on Friday – you get pocket money on Friday.

Mr A: You already owe me money for that magazine.

Daniel: You said you'd treat me!

Mr A: Did I? Oh, OK then.

Amy: That's not fair! Why don't I get a treat? You could buy me that ticket for the concert I wanted.

Mr A: That's much too expensive and anyway, I thought we were going to talk about that. It ends late and we need to know how you're getting home before we say whether or not you can go.

Amy: But when are we going to talk about it?

Mr A: We'll talk about it tonight.

COMPARE

2. Make a list of things that cause problems in the Armstrong family. Compare your list with those of other people. Now add your own ideas to the list of other issues that can cause problems in families.

FACT TO THINK ABOUT ... FACT TO THINK ABOUT ... FACT TO THINK ABOUT ...

Every year, hundreds of children – some as young as nine – leave home because of family problems and arrive on the streets of major cities in Britain.

KEY WORDS | abuse   pressure   talking it through

3. Class 7Y uses a problem/advice board. Any student can write down a family problem and pin it to the board. Other students can then write suggestion for dealing with the problem. Write answers for some of the problems below.

> I hate my brother. He always gets his own way and I always get the blame. I even have to take him with me when I go out with my friends. I've tried complaining but Dad just says we should learn to get on better.

> My granny is very ill.

> My mum's new boyfriend gives me the creeps. He's always grinning and putting his arm around me. I don't like it.

> I never seem to see my dad. He leaves home at seven, gets back after nine and is too tired to do anything with me at the weekend.

> My parents never read my homework diary or come to parent evenings. They don't seem to care how I do at school.

4. Write down one piece of advice that could go at the top of the board as an overall slogan for dealing with family pressures.

5. All families have problems at some time and they can be serious. Every year, thousands of young people, some as young as nine, run away from home because of problems. Brainstorm all the people and places you could go to for help if you had any kind of family problem, large or small.

BRAINSTORM

6. Barnardos is one organisation that works to tackle family problems such as abuse, homelessness and poverty. Their work is organised around six 'building blocks' that they believe every child needs in order to build a positive future. Discuss what each of the building blocks below might mean. Then choose one block and create a collage of words and pictures showing that building block in action.

DISCUSS

| A family that can cope. | Opportunities to learn. | Emotional, physical and mental health. |

| Protection from harm. | A sense of belonging. | A voice in society. |

Change and loss

Objective
- *To explore change and loss, and the emotions these can cause.*

CONSIDER

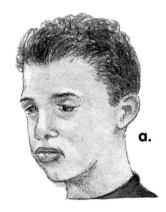
a.

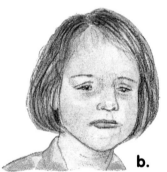
b.

c.

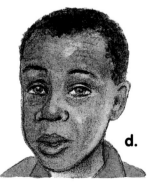
d.

1. Read the comments below. In each case, talk about what has been lost and why it caused sadness and pain.

a. "When our dog died I cried a lot. I still miss him."
b. "My granny was ill for a long time so when she died people said it was for the best, but it still hurt."
c. "We moved house when I was ten. It took me a long time to get used to a new area."
d. "I left my toy cat at the hotel and I never got him back. People laughed because I was upset but I've had that cat since I was born."

2. Any kind of loss usually brings some kind of change with it. Look back at the comments and list the changes that each loss might have brought.

3. Natalie was deeply affected by moving house, although she eventually settled and made new friends. Read the poem she wrote about moving. What emotions does she describe? What might help a person in this situation?

At first when they told me
I didn't believe it.
It wasn't true
How could it be true?
It happened to other people
Like Robert in my class
But not to me.
I felt lost and unloved, heartbroken and dazed.
200 miles – "It's not far," they said, "and you can visit."
200 miles – it's a long way to visit and it's really far.
When I left on that moving day I felt as if I would die.
I didn't cry.
I was too numb to cry.
I felt as if someone had died – was it me?

FACT TO THINK ABOUT ... FACT TO THINK ABOUT ... FACT TO THINK ABOUT ...

Research suggests that talking about loss helps people to accept and understand it.

KEY WORDS	loss grief change

4. Think of a loss you have suffered. What changes did it bring? How did you feel at the time? How do you feel about it now? Write a poem about your loss and the effects it had on you.

CONSIDER

5. After a loss, people often feel a mix of emotions. They might feel numbness, shock, feelings of helplessness, disbelief, anger, guilt, depression and a feeling of lack of direction. Eventually, most people find they gradually learn to live with the loss. Which emotion might each of the people below be feeling? What other things might someone suffering a loss think?

It shouldn't have happened.

This can't be real.

Why didn't I do things differently?

I can't bear this.

I still remember the good times.

6. It can be difficult to know what to say to someone who has suffered a loss. Imagine that a friend of yours has recently suffered a serious loss. Write down one or two suitable comments that you could make to your friend. Discuss them.

DISCUSS

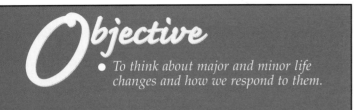

Life changes

CONSIDER

1. Read the comments below. For each one, list the emotions that the person might have felt. Remember – the person might have had 'mixed feelings'.

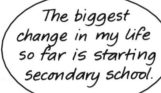

> The biggest change in my life so far is starting secondary school.

> I used to share a bedroom with my sister but now I've got a room of my own.

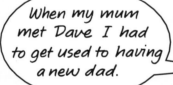

> When my mum met Dave I had to get used to having a new dad.

> I can remember my brother being born.

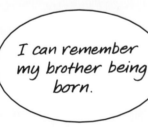

2. The first major change that happens to everyone is being born. After that, we go on experiencing big and small changes throughout life. Make a list of changes that have happened to you from birth to the present day. You can include major (big) and minor (small) changes.

FACT TO THINK ABOUT ... FACT TO THINK ABOUT ... FACT TO THINK ABOUT ...

In a recent survey, 72% of children asked said that moving to secondary school was the biggest change they had experienced in their lives.

KEY WORDS	change accepting adapting growing up

3. Create your own life map by dividing a piece of paper into squares, like a snakes and ladders board. The first square represents your birth and the last square is today. Write or draw each of your life changes into a square, and for each change write one word in the square that sums up your feelings about that change.

4. Show your life map to a partner and explain why you chose some of the words that summed up your feelings.

DISCUSS

5. The proverbs 'A change is as good as a rest' and 'Better the devil you know' mean almost opposite things. What do you think each one means and when might each one be true?

CONSIDER

Objective
● To begin looking at the physical and emotional changes that happen during puberty.

Puberty – it happens to us all

CONSIDER

1. Read the two accounts by Amy and Alex below. List the changes that happened to each of them.

I was frightened at first because I started growing hair under my arms and around my genitals. My breasts started to swell and Mum took me to buy a bra. I was getting spotty and feeling really moody and fed up. Dad said I was a right pain sometimes. Then at school one day I started my periods. I knew I would start but I was still shocked and I went to my Head of Year. She was really nice and said, "Welcome to the world of women." That made me feel really good.

I can never tell when my periods will come but Mum says that's normal at first. It can be annoying but so what? It's good growing up because you are allowed to do more things than when you were a child. My dad worries though, and says it's hard for him to see me as a young woman.

It was funny. I was quite small and suddenly I started to grow and my trousers were too short and my dad said "Here we go!". My voice was bad and it was really high and squeaky one minute and then really deep. Everyone in the class used to laugh at me. Then there was the hair – all over it seemed. My penis and testicles were growing and I wondered how big they would get! I started getting really big erections any time and at night I often woke up to find that I'd had a wet dream.

I got spots and felt on top of the world one minute and really fed up the next. Sometimes I was really rude. The first time I shaved I felt great until Dad said he'd seen more hair on a strawberry. Puberty isn't bad. I can think of worse things – like supporting Newcastle.

FACT TO THINK ABOUT ... FACT TO THINK ABOUT ... FACT TO THINK ABOUT ...

One testicle usually hangs lower than the other to stop them from being crushed when walking.

KEY WORDS	period menstruation tampons sanitary towels wet dreams masturbation erection

DISCUSS

2. Working in a small group, talk about what Amy and Alex said, and write down any question you have about the things they talked about. Share your questions as a class and find out the answers by research or by asking someone reliable.

3. The sentences below have been cut in half and mixed up. Match the correct halves together.

1. Puberty is controlled by
2. Testosterone causes the growth of the
3. Many girls have breasts that are
4. Breasts can be slightly painful
5. Women usually have two
6. The fallopian tubes are about
7. Boys start to develop facial
8. When a man ejaculates, about

a. unequal in size.
b. penis and testicles.
c. as wide as a strand of spaghetti.
d. 400 million sperm pump out of his penis.
e. hair between 14 and 16.
f. hormones that are chemical messengers.
g. just before a period.
h. ovaries.

ALL CHANGE

where to get help and advice

BRAINSTORM

4. Sometimes young people worry about puberty or have problems that they think are unusual. Brainstorm a list of people, places and organisations where young people could go to for advice and information on things to do with puberty.

5. Produce a leaflet about the physical and emotional changes that happen during puberty, including where to go for help and advice.

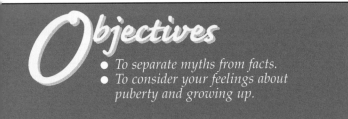

Objectives

- To separate myths from facts.
- To consider your feelings about puberty and growing up.

Puberty – myths and facts

1. Begin by doing the quiz below. Check your answers in class.

TRUE OR FALSE?

1. A man with big feet will have a big penis.
2. A girl cannot swim or wash her hair when she has a period.
3. Periods are very painful.
4. Girls lose about a bucketful of blood during a period.
5. If a boy has a small penis he won't be able to have proper sex.
6. During puberty you sweat more than usual.
7. Boys can get an erection at any time of the day or night.
8. At puberty you become moody and emotional.
9. Masturbation is harmful.
10. Puberty means you are ready to have sex.

CONSIDER

2. Where do you get information about puberty from? Which of these are reliable sources? (In other words – are likely to give you true facts.)

FACTS TO THINK ABOUT ... FACTS TO THINK ABOUT ... FACTS TO THINK ABOUT

For girls, the physical changes of puberty can begin any time between the ages of nine and sixteen.
For boys, the physical changes of puberty can begin any time between the ages of ten and seventeen.

KEY WORDS | puberty adolescence emotional physical sex

3. Look at Lisa and Daniel. Just by looking at them, how can you tell they are growing up and entering puberty? Think about their clothes and what they are doing, as well as how they look.

DISCUSS

4. Now draw either Lisa or Daniel just getting out of the shower with no clothes on. What signs can you see now that tell you they are growing up?

5. Under your picture, write a comment from Lisa or Daniel saying how they feel about puberty and growing up. Remember – they may have mixed feelings.

6. Now write your own name and your own comment describing how you feel about puberty and growing up.

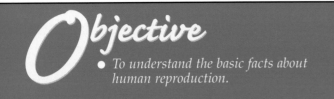

Human reproduction

Objective
● *To understand the basic facts about human reproduction.*

DISCUSS

1. For a baby to grow, a sperm from a man has to meet an egg from a woman. This is called conception. Your looks and personality are partly determined by the information carried in that egg and sperm. If a different sperm or egg had joined, you would be a different person! The statements below explain how a baby is formed. Read each statement and discuss what it means. Then use the statements and your own diagrams to produce a flow chart showing how a baby begins.

- Eggs are stored in the woman's ovaries. Sperm is made in a man's testes (also called testicles).
- When a man becomes sexually aroused, his penis becomes hard. This is called an erection.
- When a woman becomes sexually aroused, the vagina releases fluid that lubricates the area.
- During sexual intercourse, the penis moves in the woman's vagina.
- Movements of the penis in the vagina lead to ejaculation, where a creamy fluid called semen comes from the penis into the woman's vagina.
- Semen contains thousands of sperm.
- Some of the sperm swim through the woman's cervix, through the womb (also called the uterus) and up the fallopian tubes.
- If the sperm meet an ovum (egg) they gather round it. Once one sperm has entered the egg to fertilise it, the other sperm die.
- The fertilised egg moves down the fallopian tube into the womb where it may settle into the lining of the womb and begin to grow.

FACT TO THINK ABOUT ... FACT TO THINK ABOUT ... FACT TO THINK ABOUT ...

A baby develops from a single cell at conception to a human being containing about 200 million cells.

KEY WORDS   conception   intercourse   sperm   ovum

2. The people below are asking questions that people often ask about sex and conception. Find out the answers to their questions through discussion or research.

RESEARCH

What happens to the sperm that die?

Does sexual intercourse hurt?

Does a woman get pregnant every time she has intercourse?

How does a woman know she is pregnant?

3. Write down any question you wish to ask about sex and conception and pass them to your teacher. Your teacher can read some of them out and answer them with the class.

4. The period of time from conception to birth is about nine months. During that time, the growing baby relies on its mother for food and oxygen. Brainstorm the things a pregnant mother should do to give a growing baby the best chance of developing healthily.

BRAINSTORM

Keeping healthy

CONSIDER

1. List everything you have eaten in the last 48 hours. Beside each item write either 'H' for healthy or 'U' for unhealthy. What percentage of your eating was healthy?

PLAN

2. Nutritionists and doctors often talk about a healthy diet. No one food is particularly bad for you, and no one food is magically healthy. What is important is that, overall, you eat a wide combination of nutritious foods. The diagram below shows the latest ideas about what makes a healthy diet. Using the diagram to help you, plan a day's menu for a family of four. You may have to think about when they eat together and when they eat apart.

A healthy diet should contain about 12% protein, 58% carbohydrate and 30% fat.

Protein forms the cell tissue for growth and repairs to the body.

Carbohydrates give the body fuel to work and play. They can be in the form of starches or sugars. Sugars are burned up more quickly, starches provide fuel for longer. Too few carbohydrates can leave a person feeling tired and lacking in energy.

Fat also provides energy and carries some important vitamins. Most Westerners eat too much fat.

KEY WORDS	diet nutrition couch potato

3. Healthy eating is one part of healthy living but another important element is exercise. List all the exercise you have had in the past week. Include walking, dancing or any other activity that keeps you moving actively for more than ten minutes at a time.

4. Research shows that people tend to get less exercise after they leave school. Why do you think this is?

CONSIDER

5. Design a poster showing the importance of exercise and encouraging young people to take regular exercise.

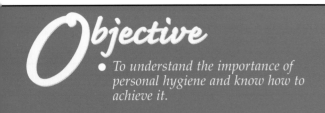
Keeping clean

CONSIDER

1. Read the stories below. How do you think people might react to Jenny and Jack? What advice would you give them?

Jenny gets up late and doesn't have time to wash. She cleans her teeth when she is going somewhere important. She showers once a week, or less, if she can get away with it. Some nights, she sleeps in her clothes to save having to dress in the morning.

She uses lots of hairspray and mousse, and washes her hair once a week, at the same time as she changes her underwear. She doesn't put her clothes out to be washed. She wears many different shoes and trainers but the same pair of socks for days on end.

Jack thinks that men don't wash. He spends a lot of time in front of the mirror squeezing spots but never cleans his fingernails. He often scratches various parts of his body. His feet smell bad – he says this shows he's a man.

He plays sport but never showers afterwards. He usually leaves it a term or more before taking his PE kit home to be washed. He cleans his teeth with his finger and cold water.

FACT TO THINK ABOUT ... FACT TO THINK ABOUT ... FACT TO THINK ABOUT ...

Sweat has no smell of its own. The stale bacteria left on the skin when sweat dries causes the smell.

KEY WORDS   acne   deodorant   dandruff

2. Look at the different parts of the body labelled below. For each one, list the personal hygiene steps that would need to be taken and say roughly how often they should happen. The armpits have been done to get you started.

LIST

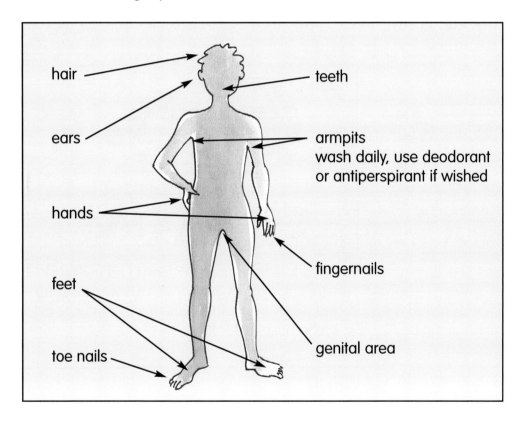

hair

ears

hands

feet

toe nails

teeth

armpits
wash daily, use deodorant
or antiperspirant if wished

fingernails

genital area

3. Imagine you work for a charity that runs a children's home for people of about your age. Many of the children have been living on the streets and know nothing about health or hygiene. You have been asked to put together a kit of basic equipment that they will need to keep themselves clean. Describe what you would include in the kit and produce a leaflet to be included, giving full instructions for personal hygiene. You should use diagrams and pictures to help make your points.

PLAN

4. Companies make huge amounts of money because people want to keep clean. Think of some adverts for personal hygiene products you have seen. What claims do they make? Are these claims true? How do you decide what to use when there are so many products on offer?

CONSIDER

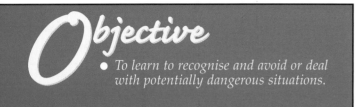
Personal safety

CONSIDER

1. What are the greatest dangers facing your age group? Why do young people sometimes take risks?

2. The people below have all been victims. For each one, suggest things they could have done that would have kept them out of danger.

Jo

"I was on the bus going home one evening. There was no one else there except a teenage girl. When the bus stopped she punched me, grabbed my purse and jumped off the bus before I knew what had happened."

Cara

"I was late for school. I couldn't find my cycle helmet so I didn't bother with it. I was hurrying and when a car stopped in front of me I hit it. I was in hospital for three weeks."

Sean

"I didn't have any money left for the taxi home and I thought Mum would have a go at me if I phoned her, so I decided to walk. A man followed me into the alley and pulled a knife on me. When I said I had no money, he cut my arm and ran off."

Greg

"I was on my own in the house one Saturday when a man knocked on the door. He said he was from the gas company investigating a leak. He told me to wait outside while he made sure it was safe. Then he stole some money, a camera and some CDs. I didn't even realise until later."

One in ten girls has experience of some kind of sexual harassment or sexual assault before they are 18.

KEY WORDS	vulnerable risk sexual harassment rape

3. Sometimes, despite our best efforts, we find ourselves in dangerous situations that we couldn't have avoided. Read the situations below. What are the dangers? Brainstorm ways of dealing with each situation.

BRAINSTORM

a. Your friend's parents are supposed to be taking you home from a school Christmas disco but you've argued with your friend and he's gone home without you.

b. You have been babysitting. Usually the children's mother runs you home but tonight the father has said he will take you. You don't feel happy about going in the car with him.

c. Your new friend called round and you went out together. Now you find yourself hanging around the playing field with a group of people you don't really know. Some of them have been drinking. They're getting loud and throwing bottles at the community hall.

4. Write a scene for a soap opera where a young person gets into a dangerous situation. Show how they deal with it and what happens as a result. You could base your scene on some of the ideas you have discussed in this lesson.

5. Write five golden rules that will help people of your age to keep safe.

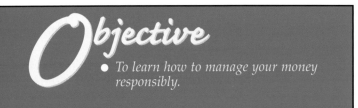
Managing your money

1. Tony has drawn a pie chart to show how he spends his money. Draw a pie chart for Sandra.

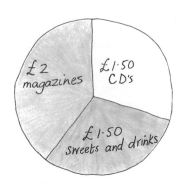

£2 magazines

£1.50 CD's

£1.50 sweets and drinks

I get £5 a week. I spend about £2 on magazines, I save £1.50 to buy CDs and the rest I spend on sweets and drinks.

I get £60 a month, but that has to cover my bus fares. I spend about £20 on bus fares, £15 on clothes and make-up, about £15 on CDs and tapes and the rest on going out.

2. Now draw a pie chart to show how you spend your money.

COMPARE

3. Most people have to save up if they want to buy something expensive. You can save at home in a money box, or use a bank, building society or post office account. List the advantages and disadvantages of saving at home and of saving in an account.

FACT TO THINK ABOUT ... FACT TO THINK ABOUT ... FACT TO THINK ABOUT ...

Children can open bank accounts and take out money from the age of seven.

KEY WORDS   bank   building society   savings account   incentive

CONSIDER

4. Many banks and building societies like to attract young customers, in the hope that they will keep these customers' accounts as they grow older and earn more money. They often offer 'incentives', which are gifts or special offers to encourage young people to open an account. Look at the two adverts for banks below. Which one would you open an account with? Why?

MIDWEST
B A N K   L I M I T E D

Give us your money and we'll give you some back!

When you open an account with us, we give you £15 in tokens, which you can spend at

BURGERLAND   **trendygear**

CLARION CINEMAS

We'll also give you a cashcard, monthly statements and 0.1% interest on money in your account.

SOUTHERN BANK

£20 OVERDRAFT   **FREE** BANKING   **0.1%** INTEREST

We don't offer worthless gifts, just worthwhile guarantees. When you open an account with us we guarantee you:
- your own chequebook and cash card
- free banking if you stay in credit
- an automatic £20 overdraft
- 0.1% interest on your money, rising to 0.15% on any money over £500.

Now that's worth having!

YOU'RE QUIDS IN WITH SOUTHERN

RESEARCH

5. When you open an account you may be offered any of the things shown below (although young customers are not usually given all of these things). Find out about each one and design a leaflet for young people explaining how each item is used.

cashpoint card   cheque guarantee card   chequebook

monthly statement   paying in book   building society pass book

*O*bjective
● *To explore negotiation and compromise as tools for solving conflict.*

Resolving personal conflict

CONSIDER

1. A conflict is a situation where people disagree. What are the conflicts in the situations below?

ROLE–PLAY

2. Working in pairs, choose one of the situations and role-play it for a short time.

3. How did your role-play develop? Did it turn into an argument or were you able to sort out the problem? Now role-play one of the other situations, but this time try hard to come to some agreement.

FACT TO THINK ABOUT ... FACT TO THINK ABOUT ... FACT TO THINK ABOUT ...

Three young people attempt suicide or harm themselves badly every hour in Britain. Much of this is as a result of unresolved personal conflict, such as relationship problems.

KEY WORDS	conflict negotiate persuade compromise

4. As a class, share some of the role-plays from the last activity. Try to spot examples of the following techniques being used.

> **Negotiation:** Trying to reach an agreement by reasonable discussion.

> **Persuasion:** Getting someone else to see your point of view.

> **Compromise:** Reaching agreement by both sides giving in a bit in order to meet the other 'half way'.

5. Now invent your own conflict situation and carry out a role-play using negotiation, persuasion and compromise to reach an agreement.

6. What things would you not compromise over?

> CONSIDER

Emergency!

CONSIDER

1. When you are faced with an emergency, your pulse rate goes up, you breathe faster and you may feel panicky. Under these conditions, it can be difficult to decide what to do quickly. Because of this, it is a good idea to think ahead so that, if you are ever faced with an emergency, you stand a better chance of dealing well with it. The box below shows the three golden rules of dealing with any emergency. For each rule, say why it is important and what might happen if you ignored it.

> **Golden rules for any emergency**
> 1. Get yourself safe and keep yourself safe.
> 2. Summon help.
> 3. Help others only if you can do so without putting yourself in danger.

2. Imagine you have just walked in to the garden shown below. In groups, decide what actions you would take, and in what order you would take them.

COMPARE

3. Compare your group's plan with those of other groups. Did you all keep the three golden rules?

FACT TO THINK ABOUT ... FACT TO THINK ABOUT ... FACT TO THINK ABOUT ...

Every year, thousands of hoax calls are made to the emergency services.

KEY WORDS	casualty emergency emergency services

4. Brainstorm all the ways you can get help in an emergency. (Hint – think of different places you might be, such as on a beach, in a shopping centre and so on.)

BRAINSTORM

5. Thinking about emergencies is one way of being prepared for them. Make a list of other things you could do that would help you deal with emergencies. Use the pictures below to help you start your list.

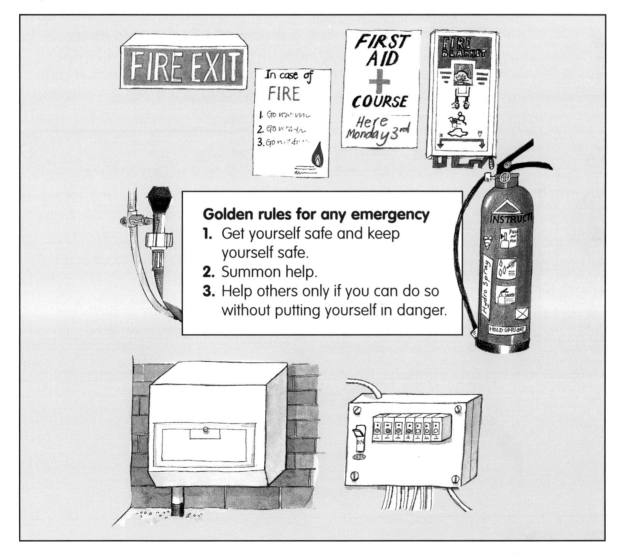

Golden rules for any emergency
1. Get yourself safe and keep yourself safe.
2. Summon help.
3. Help others only if you can do so without putting yourself in danger.

6. In groups, put together a tableau (still scene) of an emergency situation. Show each tableaux one at a time and, as a class, discuss what action should be taken.

DISCUSS

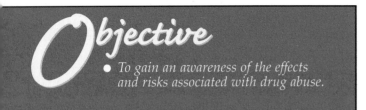

What does it do?

CONSIDER

1. Look at the list of drugs below. Which ones are legal and which ones are illegal? Which ones can be bought in a shop? Which one can only be obtained if a doctor prescribes it to you?

| Heroin Cannabis Ecstasy Aspirin Alcohol |
| Penicillin Cocaine Nicotine Caffeine |

PLAN

2. Cannabis and Ecstasy are both drugs that young people often come into contact with. Sniffing solvents is another common form of drug misuse among young people. A solvent is a strong-smelling chemical found in things like glue, aerosol sprays and lighter fuel. Working in a small group, use the information from the chart below to plan a quiz on drug abuse with ten questions.

Cannabis

Also called pot, grass, weed, marijuana, hash, dope, ganja, blow.

What it looks like
Dried leaves that can be smoked. Cannabis resin, which is a solid black or brown block, is a stronger form of the drug.

What it does
Can make you feel relaxed and talkative. Slows reflexes. If smoked with tobacco, carries the same risks as smoking. Some people feel anxious or get panic attacks.

The risks
Because reflexes are slower and it is difficult to concentrate, it would be dangerous to ride a bike or drive.

Why do you think cannabis has so many street names?

FACT TO THINK ABOUT ... FACT TO THINK ABOUT ... FACT TO THINK ABOUT ...

Every year, about 100 young people die as a result of solvent misuse.

KEY WORDS legal drug illegal drug solvent misuse cannabis ecstasy

Ecstasy

Also called many other names, including 'E', doves, Dennis the Menace, M25s.

What it looks like
Can come as tablets or capsules.

What it does
Causes alertness and rush of energy, which can be followed by a feeling of calmness and increased awareness of surroundings. Makes sound and vision feel different. It may cause a 'sick' feeling or a stiff jaw.

The risks
Raises blood pressure and causes a dry mouth. Users can exhaust themselves and need to rest, have a chance to cool down slowly, and sip water – about a litre every hour. Ecstasy kills a number of users every year.

Solvent misuse

Also called glue sniffing.

What it looks like
Any item containing solvents, such as glue, lighter fuel, aerosols or nail varnish remover. Users may sniff the substance directly from the container, or from a paper or plastic bag.

What it does
Makes you feel light-headed and drunk. Slows your breathing and heart rate.

The risks
Sniffing from plastic bags can cause suffocation if there is not enough oxygen in the bag. Aerosols sprayed into the mouth can freeze airways and prevent breathing. It could cause unconsciousness, sickness and choking to death. It may encourage risk-taking, such as stepping into the road without looking. Solvent misuse kills a number of users every year.

3. Swap your quiz with another group and challenge each other to answer the questions. (When answering the questions, do not have any information in front of you.)

4. List the reasons why people use illegal drugs.

5. For each reason on your list from question 4, give advice to someone using illegal drugs for that reason.

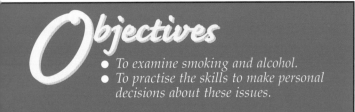

Objectives
- To examine smoking and alcohol.
- To practise the skills to make personal decisions about these issues.

Standing up for yourself

BRAINSTORM

1. Brainstorm reasons why people smoke. The pictures below may give you some ideas.

2. Working in a small group, write lists showing reasons to smoke and reasons not to smoke.

CONSIDER

3. Compare your lists with those of other people. Given the overwhelming evidence that smoking can kill you, why do people still do it?

In the United Kingdom, about 13 people die every hour because of a smoking-related disease, and about 25 000 deaths a year are alcohol related.

KEY WORDS	nicotine alcohol passive smoking drunk

4. Alcohol is another drug that can do harm. In some areas of the UK, 60% of boys and 40% of girls aged 13 to 14 drink alcohol at least once a week. Why do many young people drink? Is the pressure to drink alcohol more or less than the pressure to smoke?

DISCUSS

5. In pairs, role-play a scene where one person is trying to get the other person to smoke or drink, and the other person is trying to refuse.

ROLE–PLAY

6. As a class, share some of your role-plays. Make a list of the phrases used to try to persuade people to smoke or drink. Then, next to each phrase, write down an answer someone could use to refuse.

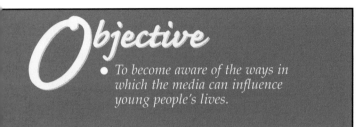

Objective
● To become aware of the ways in which the media can influence young people's lives.

Media influences on your life

DISCUSS

1. Communication is about sending and receiving messages. The method we use to communicate is called the 'medium' and the plural of the word medium is 'media'. When we talk about 'the media' we usually mean newspapers, television, movies, radio and so on.

   Working in a small group, take one minute each to talk about the forms of media you watch, read or listen to most, and give examples. For example, if you read magazines, give the names of the ones you read most often.

CONSIDER

2. Gina and Paul have each described themselves in a way that shows how the media influences them. Do you think they allow the media to influence them too much?

Gina

My hairstyle is similar to my favourite TV presenter's hair. I bought some make-up recommended by a magazine. I like clothes like the ones worn by girl bands. I'm vegetarian because of programmes I've seen about animal cruelty. I eat snacks labelled 'low fat'. I buy music I hear on cable TV. I want to work abroad after seeing a documentary about a ski resort.

Paul

I dress in a sporty style like some famous people. I buy Nike trainers, which are endorsed by my favourite athlete. I have a paper round so I can afford to go to the cinema and other places. I always drink Coke, never supermarket own brands. I've never seen Arsenal play in real life but I support them through the media. From what I have seen on the news, I am against football violence. I use an advertised spot cream.

FACT TO THINK ABOUT ... FACT TO THINK ABOUT ... FACT TO THINK ABOUT ...

Mobile phone companies are targeting children as young as six to get them to persuade their parents to buy them mobile phones.

KEY WORDS	media mass media influence

3. You may feel that the media doesn't influence you as much as it does Gina and Paul, but you are probably influenced in some ways. Would your life be exactly the same if you never saw or heard any radio, television, books, magazines or computers? Draw a diagram of yourself showing how the media influences you. The ideas in the box may help you to think about some of the areas you need to include.

> clothes   shoes or trainers   food   sweets   drinks   opinions
> hairstyle   make-up   what to buy   music to listen to
> places to go   ways of talking   career plans

4. Media influence may be good or bad. Read the comments below, then write a short magazine article for a teenage magazine about the dangers of letting the media influence us too much. You could make up examples of interviews showing how some people have been harmed by the media.

I started drinking heavily because it seemed to be the 'in' thing to do – all the famous stars did it.

My son spends a fortune on trainers because he says he has to have the right brands.

I won't travel on trains any more after seeing news reports about two train crashes.

5. The Internet has become the mass media tool and many parents worry about the things their children might find on it. Write down three rules you would make about your children using the Internet if you were a parent and explain why you would have those rules.

CONSIDER

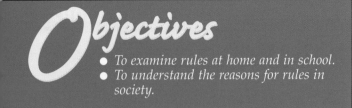

Objectives
- To examine rules at home and in school.
- To understand the reasons for rules in society.

Rules to live by

1. In pairs, take it in turns to explain one of your school rules to the other person and say what the rule is for.

CONSIDER

2. As a class, decide which school rules are most important. What happens to people who break them?

DISCUSS

3. Most families have rules at home, although they aren't written down. Imagine you are writing to someone from a different culture who has asked you about the 'rules' in your house. Write a few paragraphs explaining some of the rules you have, why you have them and what happens to family members who break them. You probably have unwritten 'rules' with your friends as well, such as how to dress or words to use. Talk about these unwritten rules. What happens to people who don't keep them?

FACT TO THINK ABOUT ... FACT TO THINK ABOUT ... FACT TO THINK ABOUT ...

Throughout history, every society we know about has had rules for individuals to follow.

KEY WORDS | rules   laws   punishment

4. A country's 'rules' are called laws. The United Kingdom has many laws. Some laws apply to the whole of the United Kingdom but sometimes laws are different in England, Scotland, Wales or Northern Ireland. Can you think of:

CONSIDER

- one law to do with age
- one law to do with property (people's things)
- one law to do with animals
- one law to do with how you can or can't treat people?

5. You can probably think of good reasons for the laws you thought of in question 4, but what happens when a country has laws that are unfair? What would you do if the laws described below were introduced in this country?

In Germany in the 1930s, the law stated that Jewish people had to wear a yellow star on their clothes whenever they were not at home.

In South Africa in the 1970s, it was illegal for black people to sit on certain beaches.

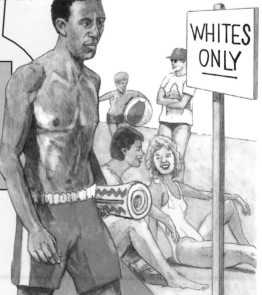

6. Who should make the laws in a society?

43

Lying, cheating and stealing

CONSIDER

1. Is it important to be honest? What would happen if no one was honest?

DISCUSS

2. Shelly has just moved to a new school. Read the cartoon and talk about why she behaved in the way she did.

3. How could each of the people in the diagram below support Shelly and help her to settle in more successfully?

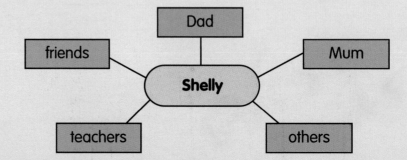

FACT TO THINK ABOUT ... FACT TO THINK ABOUT ... FACT TO THINK ABOUT ...

Every month, thousands of people are prosecuted and fined for not having a television licence.

KEY WORDS antisocial consequences fraud

BRAINSTORM

4. It is important to remember that our actions can affect people around us. When our behaviour harms or upsets people it is described as 'antisocial behaviour'. Read the news story below. Brainstorm all the people who might be affected by the boys' actions. Do you think the judge has made the right decision?

THE DAILY NEWS *Thursday 25th August 2001*

Judge names and shames young thugs

Lawrence Bagley (17) **Andrew Mendip (17)**

Look closely at these two photographs because they are the faces of two of Britain's thugs. Lawrence Bagley and Andrew Mendip were told by a judge this week that they would face up to five years in prison if they were found guilty of any antisocial behaviour within the next two years. The youths have terrorised townsfolk, including spitting, swearing and stealing. Local shopkeeper John said he dreaded seeing them, "They would upset my customers and steal whatever they could, even snatching things from people's arms." Local vicar Marion also spoke out against the boys, "On one occasion, they threw tomatoes at a wedding party who were having photos taken outside the church." Judge Kentesber placed the boys under an antisocial behaviour order yesterday, banning them from harassing or intimidating anyone in the town or causing a deliberate nuisance. In an unusual step, he also allowed the press to name the boys, saying, "The more people who recognise these boys the better. Perhaps then they will learn that this kind of vile behaviour will not be tolerated."

CONSIDER

5. Antisocial behaviour is damaging on a national level as well as being harmful to individuals. Each year, the country loses hundreds of thousands of pounds from people claiming benefits they are not entitled to. Millions more are lost through tax fraud. You may hear people argue that cheating the Government is not really stealing. Do you think this is true? What could the money be spent on in the hands of the Government?

6. Choose one type of antisocial behaviour and design a poster to persuade people against it.

Objectives

- To look at the meaning of rights and responsibilities.
- To find out about some of the groups who work to protect people's rights.

Rights and responsibilities

CONSIDER

1. As you get older, you probably have more freedom. This freedom brings responsibilities. If you have the right to choose your own clothes, then you also have the responsibility to make sure they are suitable for the occasion. If you have the right to listen to your own choice of music, then you have the responsibility to make sure it doesn't disturb other people. Make a list of other rights you think you should have and write down the responsibilities that these rights carry.

2. You may have heard the phrases 'human rights' and 'legal rights'. Read the boxes below to find out what they mean.

A human right is something that most people feel every human is entitled to. These include food, education and medical care, as well as things like fair treatment, the right to practise your religion, and free speech.

A legal right is something that is part of the law. These vary from country to country. For example, in most countries you have a legal right to keep your own possessions, so that if somebody tries to steal from you the law can punish them. In the UK, you have a legal right to a free education but this is not the case in many poorer countries.

In many countries, human rights are protected by legal rights. For example, you have a human right not to be tortured and, in most countries, this right is protected because torture is illegal.

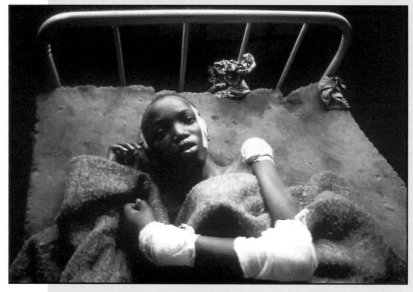

An injured war victim in Rwanda.

3. Make a list of things you consider to be human rights. How are they protected by the law?

Parents or guardians have a legal right and responsibility for taking care of their children until they are 18 years old. In extreme cases, such as cruelty or neglect, these rights can be taken away from them.

KEY WORDS	human rights legal rights responsibility

4. Some groups of people find it particularly difficult to fight for their own rights. Why might each of the groups listed in the box sometimes need help in making sure they get their rights?

5. For each of the groups in the box, list three rights that are particularly important for that group, then list the responsibilities each group should have. You may decide some groups have no responsibilities.

6. The people below work to protect the rights of others. Read their comments. In each case, whose rights are being protected? What are some of the rights of each of those groups of people?

CONSIDER

- The elderly.
- The very young.
- People with learning difficulties.
- People with a mental illness.
- Homeless people.
- People who are ill.

> I work for Scope, a national disability charity whose focus is people with cerebral palsy. We raise money to run services for individuals and support groups. We also campaign to make people understand that we should be treated equally like everyone else. We lobby politicians for laws that give disabled people rights and protect us against discrimination.

> I work for Firstbase – a local charity that runs a second-hand shop to raise money for homeless people. Wherever possible, we offer work to homeless people as well because we feel everyone has the right to a home and a way of supporting themselves.

> I belong to Amnesty International. This is an international organisation that campaigns for the freedom of prisoners of conscience. There are thousands of people all over the world who have been jailed for saying what they believe and speaking out against their governments.

7. Brainstorm other groups who work to protect people's rights. Whose rights do they protect? How do they protect them?

BRAINSTORM

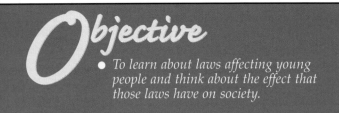
Young people and the law

CONSIDER

1. The United Kingdom's legal system has developed over hundreds of years. When new laws are added and old laws are changed, the law doesn't always seem to fit together. Look at the laws below. What ages do you think each one applies to?

> **a.** A child can buy a pet without an adult present.
> **b.** A child can drink alcohol at home.
> **c.** A young person can marry with parental consent.
> **d.** A child can be convicted of a criminal offence if the prosecution can prove he or she knows right from wrong.
> **e.** A young person can be sold cigarettes.
> **f.** A young person can vote.
> **g.** A child can be given or lent an air pistol.
> **h.** A child can be convicted of a criminal offence.
> **i.** A child can be sentenced to youth custody.
> **j.** A child can take on part-time work.
> **k.** A child must start full-time education.
> **l.** A boy can be sentenced to a detention centre.
> **m.** A child can leave school.
> **n.** A person can adopt a child.
> **o.** Girls can legally consent to sexual intercourse.

DISCUSS

2. Check your answers as a class. Are the ages appropriate? In what ways would our society be different if these laws didn't exist?

3. Look at the cases below. What laws have been broken? In each case, write down what you think should happen to the person breaking the law.

Mandy and Scott stole a car and drove it into a shop window. Mandy is 13, she was driving. Scott is 17, he was in the passenger seat.	Craig set light to his teacher's bag. He said he did it because he hated the teacher and wanted to hurt him. Craig is 10.	Eleanor punched a girl at school and broke the girl's nose. The girl's parents phoned the police. Eleanor is 16.	Jake broke into the house of a 70-year-old, threatened the owner, and stole cash and credit cards. Jake is 15.	Chandra stole two bottles of wine from a supermarket. When she was stopped by the store detective, she sprayed perfume in his face. Chandra is 14.

A dog's owner can be prosecuted for not clearing up their dog's foul on the footpath. Very few people have been prosecuted under this law so far, but local councils are beginning to use it.

KEY WORDS	adult child legal illegal custody

CONSIDER

4. Sometimes young people find themselves under pressure to break the law. Look at the conversations below. What advice would you give each of the young people? Choose one of the conversations and continue it.

5. Many laws exist to protect young people. Look at each of the laws below and write a sentence explaining how it protects young people.

- You cannot drive a car until you are 17.
- Someone under 16 cannot work before 7am or after 7pm.
- No one under 16 may work in an industrial factory.
- Teachers and youth workers have to have a police check to make sure they have not been convicted of crimes involving children before they can begin working with children.

Objective

● To gain an understanding of what 'criminal responsibility' means and explore some of the problems of juvenile crime.

CONSIDER

1. All of the news stories below are about juvenile crime. Read the articles and, for each one, suggest reasons why the person or people might have committed the crime.

Drug dealing at 12

A 12-year-old boy, who cannot be named for legal reasons, was convicted in court this week for dealing in crack and heroin. Police saw the boy cycling along the road and stopped him to find out why he was not in school. They then discovered that he was carrying sweets in one pocket, and crack, heroin and £400 in the other. After the court case, a police spokesperson told reporters, "He is the youngest drug dealer the courts have dealt with yet. I think his sentence of two years detention was well deserved."

15-year-old attacked

A 15-year-old youth, cycling home on Wednesday, was attacked by another boy of his own age. Nanthan Siva was on his way home from a youth club when another boy stepped into the road. Nanthan swerved and fell off. The other boy then kicked and punched him in the head before running off.

Dedicated shoplifters

Two 14-year-old girls were convicted of three shoplifting offences on Tuesday, and asked for a further 75 offences to be taken into consideration! Shop detectives stopped the girls as they left Top Girl late one afternoon. Police were called and discovered seven items of clothing from three different stores in the girls' bags that had not been paid for. Police later searched the girls' homes and discovered huge piles of clothing, make-up and music, which the girls admitted they had shoplifted over a period of about ten months. The court will meet again next week for sentencing.

Until the nineteenth century, children from the age of seven could be convicted of criminal offences in Britain and were often given the same punishments as adults.

KEY WORDS | juvenile   age of responsibility   crime   offence

Deadly car chase

Lives were at risk in the Birmingham area when a stolen car was spotted speeding through residential areas and along motorways in the early hours of Sunday morning. At one point, the car cut across a dual carriageway, forcing two other cars to collide.

Three people were taken to hospital and one of these is believed to have suffered a broken leg. Police finally stopped the car after a 40 minute chase, and arrested a 17-year-old man and his 16-year-old female passenger.

ROLE–PLAY

2. Choose one of the news stories. In pairs, role-play an interview for television between a television reporter and the victim, where the victim describes what happened and how he or she felt about it. (You will need to think about who the victims are in the drug dealing story.) Choose a second story and role-play another interview, making sure that you swap interviewing roles with your partner.

DISCUSS

3. Share some of your role-plays as a class. What consequences might each crime have caused? What punishment do you think each of the offenders should receive?

CONSIDER

4. In England and Wales, children can be held responsible for their actions in court at the age of ten, if the court believes that the child knows the difference between right and wrong. Before this age, it is thought that they are too young to be blamed. In Scotland, the age of criminal responsibility is 12. At what age do you think a child should be held responsible for their actions in court? Give reasons for your answer.

5. If you could speak to one of the juvenile offenders from the newspaper articles what would you say to them?

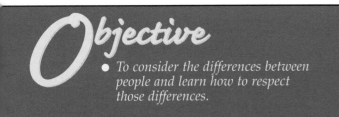
Respecting others

1. As a class, organise yourselves into a line in order of size, with the tallest at one end and the smallest at the other. When you have done that, reorganise yourselves according to age, then footsize. Record the orders in class lists.

DISCUSS

2. Talk about the differences you noticed and what this tells you about people.

3. Look at the street scene below. List the differences between the people shown. Which differences did you notice first?

KEY WORDS	respect difference understanding diversity

4. Sometimes, when people are different in some way from those around them, they can be made to feel uncomfortable. Read the comments below. How do the people feel? Produce an advice sheet for each person, giving suggestions for what they could do.

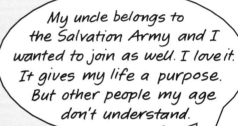

CONSIDER

> I moved to Manchester from a small village in Cornwall. People laugh at how I speak and everything is very different.

> My uncle belongs to the Salvation Army and I wanted to join as well. I love it. It gives my life a purpose. But other people my age don't understand.

> There aren't many other Muslims in the school I go to. The teachers try to be kind but they are always pointing us out. They say things like, "Why can't you be good, like Shaheen?" It doesn't help.

> I live in a very friendly village but somehow I am always made to feel different because I am the only Chinese person here. It's just little things. For example, in any discussion someone always turns to me and says, "and what do you think?" as if I must have a different opinion just because I'm Chinese.

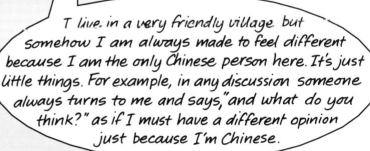

5. Produce an advice sheet for those who don't respect differences in people to help them learn respect for others.

6. "We should ignore differences between people – we are all people after all." "We should celebrate the differences between people – it's what makes us all special." Which of these statements do you agree with most? Explain your answer, using examples to make your point.

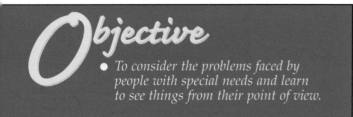

Objective
- *To consider the problems faced by people with special needs and learn to see things from their point of view.*

Whose problem?

CONSIDER

1. The dictionary describes a disability as 'a physical incapacity; a thing, or lack of something that prevents someone from doing something'. Which of the people below is disabled?

Jo works in an office where she has many friends. She lives with her boyfriend and drives a specially adapted car. The only time she needs extra help is if she visits her sister, who lives in an upstairs bedsit with no lift.

Dan finds it difficult to control his anger. He has few friends, has been divorced twice and recently lost his job because he became angry with a customer. He has just started seeing a counsellor. He says that as a child he was always made to bottle up his feelings. He feels that this has ruined his life.

FACT TO THINK ABOUT ... FACT TO THINK ABOUT ... FACT TO THINK ABOUT ...

A woman who was paralysed from the waist down after doing a parachute jump continued the sport after her accident.

KEY WORDS   disability   special needs   learning difficulty

2. Of course many physical disabilities or learning difficulties do cause people problems. But often it is the lack of facilities or understanding that causes the problem, and not the disability itself. Read the chart below. Suggest some solutions to Craig's problem. Copy the headings and continue the chart, suggesting more disabilities, problems and solutions.

Disability	Problem	Solution
Lynn is partially sighted.	She cannot read the board or most textbooks.	Lynn's teachers read out anything they write on the board and Lynn tapes it so that she can play it back. Her parents tape sections of the textbooks she uses, and a teaching assistant enlarges other sections using the photocopier. Sometimes Lynn has to ask her friends to read things for her.
David is epileptic.	He wanted to be in the school play, but the drama teacher was worried he might have a seizure during the performance.	David and another boy both learned the same part. They each performed on separate nights. On David's night, the other boy stayed backstage, ready to take over if needed.
Craig has learning difficulties.	Some people in his class laugh at him because he has to have extra help.	

3. Your school is holding a competition to find the best piece of personal writing. Each student has to write an article on their feelings, problems and worries. Imagine you are one of the people from your chart. Write an article for the competition. Remember, your feelings, problems and worries won't all be related to your disability.

4. Carry out a survey of your school to identify any problems people with disabilities might have. Suggest solutions to the problems.

RESEARCH

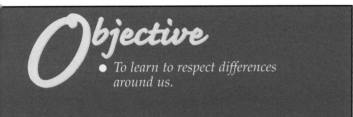

Different lifestyles

CONSIDER

1. An 'alternative lifestyle' is a lifestyle that is different from the way most other people live. Being different can take courage and most people who choose alternative lifestyles have good reasons for wanting to live that way. Look at the people below. In each case, list the advantages and disadvantages of their lifestyle.

> I've always travelled about – what people used to call gypsies. We live in caravans and vans and move around in groups, although people come and go a lot. In summer, I generally get farm work but in winter I stay nearer town and try to get work there. I would hate to stay in one place.

> The press call us 'New Age travellers' but we think of ourselves as individuals who have rejected the conventions of society. I travel about in my van, often joining protests to protect threatened areas of the countryside. I don't pay taxes because I don't agree with what the Government does with the money and I don't send my son to school because schools just turn people into machines.

> I live in a farming commune. There are six couples and eight children. Each family has its own room or rooms but we eat, work and raise the children together. We have a shop selling the fruit, vegetables and crafts we produce. Occasionally, someone will take on outside work to bring money into the community. The commune is based on a desire to create a caring and stable community for ourselves and our children.

FACT TO THINK ABOUT ... FACT TO THINK ABOUT ... FACT TO THINK ABOUT ...

Some parents choose to teach their children at home instead of in a school. The law allows this, as long as the children receive a decent standard of education.

KEY WORDS	alternative lifestyle commune traveller New Age traveller

CONSIDER

2. People often complain about those living 'alternative' lifestyles. Look at the pairs of comments below. In each case, say which comment you agree with most and why.

Travellers always leave so much rubbish behind. It's disgusting.

We do clear up a lot, but we sometimes leave some rubbish. Your dustbins are emptied every week, the council clears up after us when we've gone. What's the difference?

New Age travellers sponge off the state. They don't want to work but they still claim benefits.

If we can create a community based on respect and fairness for all, then we are doing our bit to make the world a better place.

Communes are just a way of running away from real life. They should face up to the real world and all its problems.

My work is protecting the countryside. This will benefit the whole of society so why shouldn't I claim money from the Government when I can?

ROLE–PLAY

3. Now, working in pairs, role-play an interview with a 12-year-old who belongs to one of the communities mentioned above. In your role-play you should look at the positive and negative sides of the chosen lifestyle.

4. Imagine you are taking part in a television documentary, where you spend a week with someone who lives an alternative lifestyle. Write your video diary for the week. Remember to describe your feelings as well as what you do.

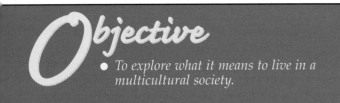

A multicultural community

Objective
- To explore what it means to live in a multicultural society.

CONSIDER

1. Read the newspaper article. What is your immediate reaction? Would it make a difference if the language being discussed was French instead of Urdu? Make a list of points for and against Stendle School teaching in Urdu.

> It's an excellent idea. It will be fairer for everyone.

> I'm not happy. My children speak Urdu, I want them to learn English.

THE DAILY NEWS   *Monday 3rd April 2001*

It's all Urdu to Me

Headteacher Jane Watson of Stendle Middle School caused outrage this week when she announced that lessons would be taken entirely in Urdu for three afternoons a week. Some parents have threatened to keep their children at home if the decision is not reversed. Ms Watson says,

"About a third of our children speak Urdu at home. The school should reflect this. All our children will benefit by becoming bilingual. Some expensive European schools teach in different languages on different days. I know it's a challenge – some of our teachers are having to learn Urdu as well!"

> It's disgusting. If they come over here they should learn English. I don't want my son jabbering rubbish.

> I'm worried in case my son falls behind, but it would be good if he could speak Urdu because many of his friends do and he sometimes feels left out.

ROLE–PLAY

2. You are going to role-play a meeting between teachers, parents, governors and children at Stendle School. Decide who you will be, and what your opinions are. Then, as a group, role-play the meeting.

FACT TO THINK ABOUT ... FACT TO THINK ABOUT ... FACT TO THINK ABOUT ...

In the UK, six per cent of the population comes from ethnic minorities. That's over three million people.

KEY WORDS	culture multicultural bilingual ethnic

3. Imagine you were a pupil at Stendle. Write a letter giving your opinions about the situation to the local newspaper.

4. Some people think that ethnic groups should keep their own culture, others think that if they live in Britain they should live in a 'British way'. Look at the opinions below. For each one say whether you agree or disagree.

CONSIDER

> Children should grow up knowing about their roots. My culture - the songs, religion, clothes, food - it's important to me. It's part of who I am. Being proud of your culture doesn't mean you can't be proud of being part of Britain too.

> It's good that people have brought their culture to Britain. I love all the wonderful foods and beautiful clothes from abroad. I've never travelled, but living in this city - it's like the world has come to me!

> There is no such thing as a 'British culture'. Young people have a different culture from older people, rich from poor, religious from non-religious. Britain has many cultures. Ethnic minorities are part of Britain, so our cultures are part of British culture too.

> People who live in Britain should try to fit in. They should learn English and wear Western-style clothes. When you're in Britain you should do as the British do.

5. If you moved to a different country, what things from your culture would you want to keep? (Think about celebrations, food, clothes, songs, language and so on.) In what ways would you try to 'fit in'?

6. Write an article with the title 'Life in a multicultural community', describing multicultural life in the United Kingdom today, and exploring the advantages and problems.

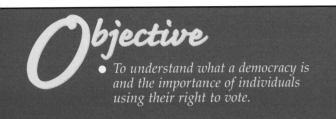

Objective

● To understand what a democracy is and the importance of individuals using their right to vote.

Having your say

BRAINSTORM

1. The box below shows the mission statement for the school council at Hitchester School. Brainstorm some of the things that might get discussed at their meetings. What things would not be discussed by the school council?

SCHOOL COUNCIL MISSION STATEMENT

The function of the school council is to:
● put forward the views of students
● take a share in the discussions concerning students
● organise events for fundraising and community awareness
● meet at regular intervals with the Headteacher to discuss matters of concern
● alert the Headteacher to any matters needing urgent attention.

CONSIDER

2. Hitchester School is about to hold school council elections. Each form must elect one person onto the council. In form 7J, the four students below are all standing for election. Read the information about them, then decide who you would vote for, and why.

Natalie enjoys sport and gets on well with people. Shy but is prepared to fight for the things that matter.	**Sean** is popular and easy going. Plays the piano. Always ready to help others.	**Rachel** is good at discussion. Has lots of friends. Sometimes in trouble for talking too much in class.	**Adam** is often seen as the class clown. Sometimes in trouble but can be very responsible and is always ready to stick up for people.

FACT TO THINK ABOUT ... FACT TO THINK ABOUT ... FACT TO THINK ABOUT ...

The Prime Minister can choose when to call a general election, but it must be at least every five years.

KEY WORDS	democracy general election Member of Parliament vote

Countries where all the adults have a say in how the country is run are called **democracies**. Usually, this works by people voting for the person they want to represent them in government. In Britain, anyone who is 18 or over (with a few exceptions) can vote in local or general elections to elect the MP (Member of Parliament) for their area. The United Kingdom is divided into 659 areas known as **constituencies** and each constituency has one MP who has been elected by the people of that area to represent them. An MP represents all the people in his or her area, not just the ones who voted for him or her. Most MPs belong to one of the big political parties – Labour, Conservative or Liberal Democrats. Some MPs belong to smaller groups, such as the Green Party and some MPs are **independent**, which means they are not members of any political party. Some parties only stand for election in individual countries, such as the Scottish Nationalists in Scotland, Plaid Cymru in Wales, the Ulster Unionists, Sinn Fein, SDLP and Democratic Unionists in Northern Ireland.

BRAINSTORM

3. Brainstorm a list of questions you might want to find out about someone before deciding whether or not to vote for them in an election. How could you find out this information?

4. Look at the opinions below. Which one do you agree with the most, and why?

CONSIDER

Voting is a waste of time. There are hundreds of thousands of people in the country. How can my one vote make any difference?

By voting, we can affect how the country is run. MPs represent our views, so it's our job to find out what we need to know in order to choose sensibly.

I don't bother to vote. I don't understand most of what they're talking about and most of it's probably lies. These politicians are all as bad as each other.

5. Put together a leaflet explaining why voting is important and encouraging people to vote.

Living in the community

COMPARE

1. In small groups, write down a definition of the word 'community'. Afterwards, compare your ideas with those of other groups.

2. Think of two communities, for example, a school and a local estate or neighbourhood. In what ways are they similar? In what ways are they different?

3. Now think about the community where you live. Write a list of all the different groups of people who live in your area. The pictures below may help you.

FACT TO THINK ABOUT ... FACT TO THINK ABOUT ... FACT TO THINK ABOUT ...

The Notting Hill Carnival began as a small community event in 1966. Now it is a huge annual event attracting thousands of visitors but still involving the local community.

KEY WORDS   community spirit   community police   community centre

4. Plan a community centre that will serve the needs of all the people in your area. Your plan should be well presented, with explanations for the decisions you have made and should include:

PLAN

- a sketch of the layout showing rooms and facilities available
- an idea of what the building might look like from the outside
- any outside facilities you want to include
- suggestions for where the centre could be built
- a name.

5. Write about the communities you are a part of. Explain how you fit into these communities and describe your role in them.

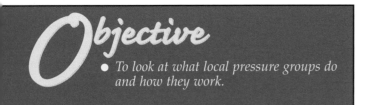

Pressure groups

BRAINSTORM

1. What places do you value locally? Imagine one of them was about to be bulldozed. Brainstorm all the things you could do to try to stop the place from being destroyed.

CONSIDER

2. Sometimes people feel so strongly about something that they get together with other people to campaign. These groups often begin with just a few people, although they can grow to be very large. People group together to campaign for many different things. What might the campaigns below be about? What other things might pressure groups campaign for?

FACT TO THINK ABOUT ... FACT TO THINK ABOUT ... FACT TO THINK ABOUT ...

'Friends of the Earth' originally started as many small groups of people in different countries who cared about the environment. There are now over 14 million members.

KEY WORDS	pressure groups lobbying

3. Read the information below about the pressure group 'Learn and Live'.

'Learn and Live' is the original pressure group, formed in 1989, committed to improving road safety, particularly among young and inexperienced drivers.

Over a thousand young lives are lost each year on UK roads. Young, newly qualified drivers are the most likely to have accidents. The chances of having an accident are almost halved after having been driving for two years.

L EARN + L IVE
The Parents Campaign
for
Safe Driving Tuition

We campaign for:
* new drivers to use 'P' plates
* driving tuition to include motorway driving, night driving and skid control
* limits on the driving of high-powered cars and the number of young passengers that can be carried
* education and publicity aimed at parents and learner or new drivers.

Our successes include persuading the Government to bring in a law stating that learner drivers must be accompanied by someone who is over 21 with at least three years driving experience.

4. Pressure groups often lobby their MPs. This means writing or talking to them to try and persuade them to put forward the group's views to the Government. Imagine that you are a supporter of 'Learn and Live'. Write to your MP asking for his or her support for your campaign, explaining why you think it is important and saying what you would like to see happen.

5. Pressure groups like 'Learn and Live' rely on people volunteering to give up their time to support a campaign. What campaigns would you be prepared to support? What would you be prepared to do to support those campaigns?

CONSIDER

The Houses of Parliament

1. The United Kingdom is run by a government. Most of the debates take place in the Houses of Parliament. There are two houses. Read the boxes below to find out about them.

The House of Commons
This is the place where Members of Parliament who have been elected sit. They debate issues and introduce new laws.

The House of Lords
For a law to be passed, the House of Lords has to agree to it, although it is very unusual for the House of Lords to reject completely a law that had already been passed by the House of Commons. In the past, anyone who was a peer (Lord or Lady) could sit in the House of Lords. Some people are made peers because they have done good work for the country, but many are peers because their parents were. This means that the House of Lords has not been an elected group. This system is currently changing and a voting system is being introduced so that the House of Lords is more democratic.

Many countries have no voting system. In others, people can 'vote' but there is only one party, and in others only some people can vote.

KEY WORDS parliament   Member of Parliament   democracy   election

2. If you listen to news broadcasts about politics, you will often hear some of the words in the box below. Match each word to its definition.

Word

Member of Parliament (MP), Speaker, Government or Governing party, Opposition, General Election, Cabinet, Prime Minister, Leader of the Opposition.

Definition

A Acts as the chairperson in the House of Commons.

B Political parties in the House of Commons that are not the governing party.

C Title given to the leader of the second largest party in the House of Commons.

D Leader of the party that wins the most seats in a general election. This person is leader of the country.

E The party that wins the most seats in a general election.

F When the electors of the country vote to select their Members of Parliament.

G A person elected by a constituency (area) to represent the people in the House of Commons.

H Group of about twenty MPs chosen by the Prime Minister to meet weekly and decide on government policy.

3. Imagine you are a political correspondent for a television company. Choose one of the topics below (or think of a topic yourself) and make up a news story about it. Try to use some of the words from question 2 in your report.

Suggested topics:
- Extra money to be made available for schools.
- Hospital waiting lists go up. Laws on upper age limits on treatment and operations to be reviewed.
- Government to introduce tax for pet owners.

Scotland has its own parliament and Wales and Northern Ireland have assemblies where many decisions are taken – England has no separate parliament.

4. Some MPs are independent, which means they don't belong to a political party. Most do belong to a party. Why do we have political parties? What would happen if we didn't?

CONSIDER

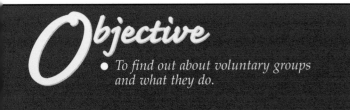

Why do they do it?

1. Many people work to help others without being asked to and without being paid. These people are called volunteers. Working in pairs, take turns to be the volunteers shown below while the other person interviews you about what you have done and why you did it.

I sat in a bath of cold porridge outside my local pub to raise money for the daughter of a friend of mine. The little girl was brain damaged at birth. She needs lots of special equipment, like wheelchairs and special toys, and people to help teach her.

After qualifying as a dentist, I spent a year working in India on a charity project to provide free dental care to people in Delhi. I felt I should give some of my time before coming back to Britain to earn a living.

2. Brainstorm all the voluntary and charity groups and charities that you know of. You could look in local newspapers and telephone directories to help you.

FACT TO THINK ABOUT ... FACT TO THINK ABOUT ... FACT TO THINK ABOUT ...

Voluntary Services Overseas currently have 1800 volunteers working on projects in many developing countries.

KEY WORDS | volunteer   local   national   international

3. Divide the groups on your list into local, national and international groups. The boxes below may help you to decide which they are.

COMPARE

Local – focused on one area.

National – working across the whole of Britain.

International – working in more than one country.

4. Working in a small group, choose three voluntary organisations: one local, one national and one international. Produce a display advertising the work of these groups and explaining why you think people should support them.

5. People who work for voluntary groups are helping others, but what do they get out of it themselves?

CONSIDER

Objective
● To understand the idea of a global community and our part in it.

A global community

1. The cartoons below may not be historically accurate, but what do they tell you about how our world has changed over the centuries? What inventions have helped bring about this change?

2. In your lifetime, you will travel many thousands of miles, and you may go abroad. Even if you never go abroad, your life will still be affected by many other countries. Look at the labels on the clothes you are wearing and any bags or equipment you have to see if you can find out where they come from. Think about the food you have eaten recently. Where might it have come from?

3. Read the comment below.

As a child, I lived in a small farming community. One year we had storms that damaged the crops. Neighbours helped each other and there was a real spirit of community. Years later, I worked on a project in South America to help homeless street children. The workers came from all over the world, but there was the same spirit of community at work. It was as if everyone belonged to one global community. I felt as if the children and the other workers were my neighbours.

FACT TO THINK ABOUT ... FACT TO THINK ABOUT ... FACT TO THINK ABOUT ...

One of the conclusions of the Brandt report of 1980, which looked at the problem of world poverty, was that 'The world is one and we must begin to act as members of it who depend on each other'.

KEY WORDS	neighbour global community

DISCUSS

4. Sally uses the expression 'global community'. In groups, talk about what it means, then write down a definition to explain 'global community'. Compare your definition with those of other groups.

CONSIDER

5. The list on the left below shows some of the things people do to help their world neighbours. The list on the right shows how these actions can help, but they are in the wrong order. Match each pair correctly.

1. Buying 'fair trade' goods.

2. Giving time, money or goods to charity.

3. Checking that wooden products come from 'managed' forests.

4. Walking or cycling instead of taking the car.

5. Reading or watching the news.

a. Wood from non-managed forests can destroy the homelands of some tribal peoples.

b. Air pollution from traffic, homes and industry contributes to the greenhouse effect, which is thought to be affecting the world's climate.

c. Being aware of what is going on in the world puts you in a stronger position to act responsibly.

d. Many charities work to help people at home and abroad.

e. Companies such as Oxfam who sell 'fair trade' goods make sure that the people who produced the goods get a fair price for them.

Pollution on the Grand Union Canal, London.

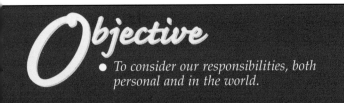

Objective

• *To consider our responsibilities, both personal and in the world.*

Every little helps

BRAINSTORM

1. Brainstorm the things people in your class are personally responsible for. (For example, dressing yourself, feeding your pet, tidying your bedroom.)

CONSIDER

2. Look at some of the things from your list. What would happen if you didn't do them?

3. When one person is responsible for something, it is obvious when it isn't done, but if more than one person is responsible for something, it becomes easier not to do it, and then to blame other people. You could argue that there is no point in trying to save the environment by walking to school if all your friends travel by car. Look at the cartoon below. What is it saying about individual and group responsibility? Write a suitable caption for each frame of the cartoon.

FACT TO THINK ABOUT ... FACT TO THINK ABOUT ... FACT TO THINK ABOUT ...

From a group of young people surveyed, 68% said they believed that they could bring about change if they worked together.

KEY WORDS responsibility individual cooperation

4. Sometimes, world problems seem too big for individuals to tackle, but it is only by individual actions that change can occur. Look at the problems below. For each one, make a list of things an individual person could do to improve the situation.

> destruction of rainforests, global warming, inequality, pollution, war, cruelty to animals.

Deforestation in Brazil.

5. Prepare a publicity campaign to make young people more aware of how they can take responsibility for world problems. Your plan should include a slogan, a song or jingle, and a script or storyboard for a three-minute video.

PLAN

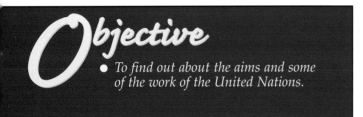

The United Nations

CONSIDER

1. In 1945, representatives from 51 countries started an organisation where different countries could work together to sort out problems peacefully. What happened that year to encourage people to look for ways of sorting out problems?

2. The countries that met formed an organisation called the United Nations. Today, 189 countries are members of the United Nations; nearly every country in the world. The central aim of the UN is to preserve world peace and improve people's lives. Look at the United Nations symbol. Write a few paragraphs explaining what the name 'United Nations' and the symbol mean.

3. The UN's work covers many different areas of life and some of these are shown below. Look at each one and suggest some of the things the UN might do in this area.

> ● Peace and security.
> ● Economic and social development.
> ● Human rights.
> ● International law.
> ● Humanitarian affairs.

Children queue for food in a Somalian refugee camp.

FACT TO THINK ABOUT ... FACT TO THINK ABOUT ... FACT TO THINK ABOUT ...

Over 1600 UN peacemakers have been killed, whilst trying to keep the peace, since 1948.

KEY WORDS | United Nations peace member nation committee

4. UNICEF is the United Nations children's fund. One of the ways UNICEF raises money is by selling greetings cards. The money is then used to provide emergency aid for children living in areas where there are famine, floods and war. Estimates suggest that UNICEF saves the lives of 400 000 children under five each year. Read the story of Amma below.

> When soldiers and rebels started fighting near my village we were trapped. The rebels were in the hills behind us and the army was coming up towards us. We could hear the shell fire all day, sometimes right in the village. The UN established a peace zone to the west of our village. They came in trucks and took us to a camp that was safe from fighting. UN soldiers patrolled the area to make sure the rebels and army kept away. We were all crammed into tiny tents and there wasn't enough food or water at first, but at least we were safe from the bullets.

5. Imagine you were a UN committee organising a 'zone of peace' for wartime refugees. Make a list of all the supplies and equipment you would need. Which six items would be the most important?

6. "Most countries are members of the UN, but there are still wars, poverty and disasters, so it's obviously a waste of time!"
Do you agree or disagree with this comment? Give reasons for your answer.

CONSIDER

For each of the people shown on pages 76–79, research why they are famous and write your judgement of them as a citizen.

Anita Roddick

Lord Shaftesbury

Odette
Churchill

Nelson Mandela

Answers

PUBERTY – IT HAPPENS TO US ALL
1f, 2b, 3a, 4g, 5h, 6c, 7e, 8d.

PUBERTY – MYTHS AND FACTS
1f, 2f, 3f, 4f, 5f, 6t, 7t, 8t, 9f, 10f.

YOUNG PEOPLE AND THE LAW
a12, b5, c16, d10, e16, f18, g14, h14, i15, j13,
k5, l14, m16, n21, o16.

THE HOUSES OF PARLIAMENT
MP – G, Speaker – A, Government or Governing
party – E, Opposition – B, General Election – F,
Cabinet – H, Prime Minister – D, Leader of the
Opposition – C.

A GLOBAL COMMUNITY
1e, 2d, 3a, 4b, 5c.

Acknowledgements

© 2001 Folens Limited, on behalf of the authors.

United Kingdom: Folens Publishers, Apex Business Centre, Boscombe Road, Dunstable LU5 4RL.
Email: folens@folens.com

Ireland: Folens Publishers, Greenhills Road, Tallaght, Dublin 24.
Email: info@folens.ie

Poland: JUKA, ul. Renesansowa 38, Warsaw 01-905.

Editor: Alison MacTier
Layout artist: James Brown
Cover design: Martin Cross
Illustrations: Kathy Baxendale, Jean de Lemos – Graham-Cameron Illustration, Keith Howard and Avril Turner – Linda Rogers Associates, Debbie Riviere
Photographs:
pages 36 George Post, 37 (top) Pascal Geotgheluck, both Science Photo Library
page 37 (bottom) Christine Moorcroft
pages 46 Paula Bronstein/Impact Visuals, 63 (bottom) Joanne O'Brien, 71 Maggie Murray, all Format Photographers
pages 63 (top left) Peter Olive, (top right) David Tothill, 66 Crispin Hughes, all Photofusion
pages 73 D Charlwood, 74 P Francis, both Tropix
page 74 (top) By permission of The United Nations
page 76 Sean McNenemy, The Body Shop
pages 77, 78, 79 Popperfoto
Text:
Learn and Live for permission to reproduce their logo

First published in 2001 by Folens Limited.
Reprinted 2001, 2002 (three times).

British Library Cataloguing in Publication Data. A catalogue record for this publication is available from the British Library.

ISBN 1 84163 834-X